THE HISTORY OF
GAELIC GAMES

Appletree Press

THE HISTORY OF
GAELIC GAMES

IAN PRIOR

Appletree Press

First published in 1997 by
The Appletree Press Ltd, 19-21 Alfred Street,
Belfast, BT2 8DL
Tel: ++44 (0) 1232 243074
Fax: ++44(0) 1232 246756
email:frontdesk@appletree.ie

A History of Gaelic Games

A catalogue record for this book is available from The British Library.

website: www.irelandseye.com

ISBN 0 -86281-663-7

9 8 7 6 5 4 3 2 1

CONTENTS

—⊷ ⊶—

—⊷ ⊶—

CROKE PARK ON ALL-IRELAND FINAL DAY

Out they stamp from the dressing room tunnel and into the sunshine where the whiff of freshly clipped grass and the roars of multitudes assault the senses. Around them, the stands and terraces explode in a cacophony of sound and bright colour as tribal banners swirl in the breeze, each one a statement of belonging, an expression of identity with home, family and friends.

For seventy minutes the teams unleash the results of months of excruciating preparation, of long runs up the steepest of hills, of practising to perfection as the chill of a winter's evening bites.

The Gaelic games of hurling, football, camogie and handball are far removed from the glittering ranks of global sport: seven figure sponsorship deals and international stardom do not beckon Gaelic players. But to win brings a sense of immortality that materialism can never provide. Amateur in their ethos, Gaelic games exist through the bonds of identity they forge among their participants and devotees. From the youngster who runs out in the colours of his native parish to the county player who stars in front of 70,000 people on All-Ireland final day in Croke Park, the reason for playing is the same. It is roughly coined as *pride in the jersey*, the oldest of mantras within Ireland's biggest sporting organisation.

The man who scores the winning goal may well be your neighbour, or live in the town five miles down the road. He is playing for the same reason that you are watching. Be it the parish, the school, or the county, the game is where you are and where your roots find their deepest grip.

Founded out of national pride, sustained through lean times with that same emotion, few things run so deeply through the core of Irish society than the connection with place and home which the games provide. In a sporting world where players change allegiances for the price of a hospital wing and satellite television holds fans to ransom, there remains in Gaelic games vital proof of a purer ideal.

chapter one

ORIGINS

In the pantheon of global sports such as soccer, rugby union or athletics, Gaelic games barely merit a footnote. The Irish have been 'hiding' their games since long before Christ walked the earth. In more modern times, Gaelic games have formally existed since the foundation of the Gaelic Athletic Association in the billiards room of a Tipperary hotel in 1884.

There, led by visionaries Michael Cusack and Maurice Davin, the first formalised codes and cohesive organisation of the ancient Irish games were initiated, and the seeds planted for what would become Ireland's largest sporting organisation.

Before the Association's foundation, Gaelic games had existed in various guises for countless centuries. Hurling in particular has its origins deep in the lore of Irish mythology, where it featured often in pre-Christian Celtic folklore.

The first mention of hurling dates back to 1272BC, when as a prelude to a battle for control of the country, the Fir Bolg and Tuatha de Danaan tribes are said to have played near Cong, county Mayo. According to the ancient Gaelic annals:

"Ruad, with twenty sons of the courageous Mil, sped westwards to the end of Mag Nia to offer a hurling contest to the Tuatha De. An equal number came out to meet them. The match began. They dealt many a blow on legs and arms until their bones were broken and bruised and they fell outstretched on the turf and the match ended".

Opposite: Stick game, similar to hurling, depicted on fourteenth century altar set

Legendary warrior Cuchulainn (literally *Hound of Cullen*) was so named after killing a fierce guard dog by driving a hurling ball down its throat. The Celtic legal system, the Brehon Laws, provided for compensation for hurling accidents and provisions were also made for cases of deliberate injury, or even death, as a result of hurling.

Such stories often portray hurling as a form of martial training and proficiency on the hurling field was equated with skill in battle. During the middle ages, hurling survived several attempts to ban it by various colonial governors who considered the game a distraction from more worthy martial pursuits such as archery or fencing. Throughout the countryside, hurling thrived as a wild and often violent practice with few set rules.

One seventeenth century account describes the game as being played on a plain about 2-300 yards long, with victory going to the first team to drive the ball through the opponent's goal. Though ostensibly a peasant recreation, the game was often an ill-disguised excuse for faction-fighting, and contemporary descriptions detail sometimes horrific injuries and riotous behaviour among the participants.

During the seventeenth century, hurling had its strongholds, in the southern half of the country. It was popular in Cork, Galway, Limerick, Tipperary and Kilkenny, with other outposts such as Antrim in the far north. To this day, these counties are traditional heartlands of hurling. There were substantial regional variations on the way the game was played, and no real attempts to form a unified code were made until around the time of the Association's formation.

The nineteenth century saw a version of hurling, or *hurley* as it was referred to, become popular with the upper classes. By 1879 there were at least six hurley clubs among the gentry in Dublin, and the Irish Hurley Union was founded in Trinity College. It was exclusively an upper-class preserve and bore little relation to traditional concepts of the game.

The extent to which this version of the game was relevant to its rural cousin is evident in one of the earliest actions of the Irish Hurley Union, which wrote to the English Hockey Union for a set of rules.

The gentrified game was seen by the Association's founders, Michael Cusack in particular, as an aberration which was in danger of converting the traditional sport to a variant of hockey.

To offer an alternative, Cusack founded the Academy Hurling Club in the early 1880s with rules based on the rural game and organised practice sessions in Dublin's Phoenix Park. These proved immediately popular, and substantial crowds marched through Dublin each Saturday morning with hurleys on their shoulders to attend.

This evolved into the Metropolitan Hurling Club, also founded by Cusack. He set out to establish links with rural clubs in the south and west which proved receptive to the idea of national competitions. After playing against a Galway team, who operated under a different set of rules, Cusack realised the need for common regulations and this inspired much of his thinking with regard to the formation of the GAA.

In the case of Gaelic football, origins are murkier. A rough-and-tumble form of the game was common throughout the middle-ages, similar versions of which abounded throughout Europe and eventually became the forebears of both soccer and rugby.

The earliest records of a recognised precursor to modern Gaelic football date from a game in county Meath in 1670, in which catching and kicking the ball were permitted.

A six-a-side version was played in Dublin in the early eighteenth century, and one hundred years later, there were accounts of games played between county sides. Before the potato famine of the 1840s which proved hugely detrimental to all Irish sports, a codified game had emerged in east Munster, but the arrival of rugby union and soccer with fixed rules caught the imagination of the upper classes and native football was in danger of dying out. A particular signpost of this decline was the speed with which the schools of the middle classes adopted and promoted the newly promoted games, particularly in Dublin, Cork and Belfast.

Limerick was a stronghold of the native game around this time, and the Commercials Club, founded by employees of Cannocks' Drapery Store, was one of the first to impose a set of rules which were adopted by other clubs in the city. Competition remained localised, with occasional friendly matches against various sides around the country. Of all the 'National Pastimes'

which the GAA set out to promote, it is fair to say that football was in the worst shape at the time of the Association's foundation.

Handball formed the third strand of Ireland's games. In the early nineteenth century it had been common throughout the country wherever a gable wall and a few yards of space were available, but in common with most popular sports, it was hard hit by the famine. The latter part of the century saw it in decline, and to this day, it has never really enjoyed the mass appeal of football or hurling.

Camogie, the women's version of hurling, began with the

formation of the first club in 1903. Early rules included a prohibition on impeding the ball with the long skirts fashionable at the time, and it took time before prejudice allowed the rules to facilitate any serious competitive edge. The Ladies' Football Association was not set up until 1974, ninety years after the formation of the original Association. In common with camogie, its ruling body enjoys autonomy from the main body of the GAA, a situation considered preferable by both sides, although strong affiliations are retained. Today, women's football is the fastest growing sport in Ireland. Camogie and women's football are played at league and championship level, with finals held in Croke Park.

From meagre beginnings, the modern GAA grew. Statistics show that upwards of a million people attend the intercounty football and hurling championships each year. As well as over 2600 separate clubs in Ireland, there are branches in England, Scotland, USA, Australia and Canada. The Association is the landlord of thousands of acres in Ireland and beyond and rakes in a surplus stretching well into seven figures annually.

Though rules of play have evolved considerably from early incarnations, both football and hurling are now played between teams of 15-a-side. A point is scored by placing the ball over the crossbar, while a goal is worth three points.

In hurling, each hurler plays with a *camán*, a curved stick made from ash wood, about three and a half feet in length. Hurlers seek possession of a tennis size leather ball, known as a *sliotar*.

The principal competitions are the All-Ireland series, known as the Championship, which culminates in the hurling and football finals each September. County sides compete on a knock out basis within each of the four provinces, with one qualifier from each province contesting the semi-finals. Recently, however, the rules for the hurling championship have been modified whereby the losers from the Leinster and Munster finals are re-admitted to face the Ulster and Connacht champions at a quarter-final stage. This came about mainly because of a gross imbalance in strength in the south and east of the country.

Football's top prize is the Sam Maguire Cup, named after a London-born revolutionary and Gaelic games enthusiast, while hurling's equivalent is the Liam McCarthy Cup.

Second to the Championship comes the National League, the football version of which is played out during the winter months. Since 1997, the hurling has started from March onwards to maximise the chances of dry ground to which the game is suited.

The early stages of the National League are run off on a divisional basis for both football and hurling with four divisions in each sport. The top teams from each division then qualify to play in quarter-finals and so on until the league champions have been decided. These competitions are mirrored at club level, where each county has its own league and championship. The winners of individual county championships go on to contest provincial and All-Ireland club championships, the finals of which are held in Croke Park on St Patrick's Day.

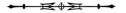

ChAPTER TWO

BEGINNINGS

The founding of the GAA in 1884 was set against a backdrop of much political turbulence. As well as the struggle for Home Rule being waged in the House of Commons by Charles Stewart Parnell and his Irish Party, there was considerable dissent in the countryside. The previous years had seen poor harvests and tenants, unable to pay the high rents imposed on them by the landlords of the ascendancy, were evicted in their thousands. Michael Davitt, a revolutionary and early patron of the GAA, organised the Land League to fight for tenants' rights to fair rent and ownership of land. Violence was widespread throughout the country. To add to this, the Irish Republican Brotherhood, also known as the Fenians, had revived and was intent on establishing itself as a credible revolutionary group.

The GAA was founded at the dawn of an era when Ireland, having emerged from the misery of the Famine years, was once again ready to assert itself both politically and culturally. Considering this climate, it is unsurprising that the early history of the Association is steeped in politics, the traces of which remain to this day.

In 1884 rugby looked well-poised to take control of organised football in Ireland. It had gained rapid acceptance among the middle classes, and perhaps more importantly, among the better secondary schools. Irish games at the time were so disorganised and sporadic as to be in danger of complete extinction. A great deal of the credit for this being

prevented goes to two men: Michael Cusack and Maurice Davin.

A fluent Irish speaker, Cusack was a native of the Burren in county Clare, an area with strong hurling traditions. A fine athlete in his time, he played hurling from an early age and also dabbled with rugby. Having trained as a teacher in Dublin up until 1871, he was appointed principal of a primary school in Galway. From there he graduated to numerous teaching posts around the country before settling in Dublin in the late 1870s, where he met and married Margaret Woods. The couple were comfortably off, with Cusack opening up an academy which specialised in preparation for police and civil service examinations.

Politically, Cusack was an avowed separatist. Strong-willed to the point of stubbornness, he was an accomplished debater who relished the challenge of an argument. His charisma was such as to naturally single him out for leadership, and he was not of a temperament for taking orders. This was to stand him in good stead when he resisted attempts to make the GAA a lackey of the independence movement in its early years. Were it not for his original vision and single-mindedness, it is unlikely that the Association would ever have endured.

If Cusack was the man with the master plan, it was the pragmatic guidance of Maurice Davin which nurtured the Association through its stormy early years. Davin, who came from Carrick-on-Suir in Waterford, was Ireland's most famous athlete of the time. His youth had been devoted to boxing and rowing - it is said that he never lost a race in a boat of his own

[Established over a Century.]

THE COMMERCIAL AND FAMILY HOTEL,

AND POSTING ESTABLISHMENT,

THURLES.

LIZZIE J. HAYES, Proprietress.

construction. In later life he turned to athletics and broke many of the existing records for throwing and jumping competitions. The early GAA was as much concerned with athletics as the more traditional Irish games, and someone of Davin's fame gave it considerable sporting prestige. Although still in his early forties at the time the Association was set up, he was already regarded as a 'Grand Old Man' of Irish sport.

Davin was noted for his meticulous sense of fair play. One anecdote avows that when acting as a judge at a race meeting, he refused to allow a record set by his own brother stand because of the overly favourable weather conditions.

By mid-summer of 1884, Davin and Cusack's planning was reaching an advanced stage. Amid the uncertainty of the times, new organisations were ten-a-penny and most, such as the National Council, the Dungannon Clubs, the United Irish League and the People's Protection Association were purely political. Accordingly, one of the most pressing needs was to establish the support of prestigious patrons. In late nineteenth century Ireland, this meant the Catholic Church.

Approaches were made to the Archbishop of Cashel, Dr Croke, one of the more liberal clergymen of the time who was known to have a passionate interest in sport. He was more than enthusiastic, giving Cusack the impetus to convene the historic meeting in Thurles, which took place on All Saints' Day, November 1 1884.

Records as to who exactly was present in the billiards room

Archbishop Croke.

of Hayes's Commercial Hotel remain sketchy. What is known for sure is that seven people whom Cusack had publicly invited through a letter in the national press did show up. Two journalists, John Wyse-Power of the *Leinster Leader* and Willie McCay, a Belfast man who worked for the *Cork Examiner*, were elected along with Cusack as joint Honourary Secretaries after Davin was voted unanimously as the first President. The original agreed name was *The Gaelic Association for the Preservation and Cultivation of National Pastimes*, a verbose title which was quickly shortened to the *Gaelic Athletic Association*.

Others present at the meeting included James Bracken, a building contractor from Templemore who was there by virtue of his links with the Fenian movement; District Inspector Thomas McCarthy, an Royal Irish Constabulary member who left the Association soon after its foundation to pursue a career in the police force and finally, P J O'Ryan, a solicitor from Tipperary. A rousing letter of endorsement from Archbishop Croke was read out and published afterwards, winning the fledgling organisation much support among the populace. Michael Davitt, the so-called 'one-armed Fenian' and agrarian reformist was also a patron.

The Association devised rules for the games, with the first versions being published in *The United Irishman* in February 1885. Although in the first year the primary concentration was on athletics, it was hurling which caught the public imagination. The game spread rapidly in the south of the country as the traditional heartlands embraced the first coded structure of the game they had known. Elsewhere, Ballyconnell in Cavan was the first club formed in Ulster, followed quickly by Magherafelt in Derry.

But an early directive from the Association's leadership brought it into immediate conflict with the country's other sporting bodies. Cusack's view was that existing organised sports such as soccer, cricket, hockey and rugby were a threat to the development of the national pastimes. He engineered a directive in March 1885 to the effect that GAA members who participated, or actively promoted foreign games would be suspended from the Association.

The move brought outrage from the other bodies and caused immediate suspicion as to the true motives behind the GAA.

Cusack had some heated and very public exchanges with the Irish Amateur Athletic Association, which angered Archbishop Croke to the extent that he considered withdrawing his patronage. Cusack relented and the ban was done away with through compromise - individual counties were allowed to decide whether or not to enforce it. But it was nowhere near the last to be heard on the subject. After being reinstated in 1903 it was to survive an incredible fifty eight years before finally being dropped in 1971.

Internal divisions were also rife in the early years. The GAA survived an attempt by Munster counties to form a breakaway National League, and the split which occurred after Irish Party leader Charles Parnell was found to have committed adultery almost finished the Association. It was an issue which divided the Irish people, and although most of the senior figures in the

GAA came out in support of Parnell, the Church's utter condemnation of him weighed heavily with the grass roots. Apathy set in, and by 1893 the Association was heavily in debt. At the Annual Convention that same year, only Dublin, Cork and Kerry sent official delegations. It was due to the unifying efforts of Maurice Davin and President P J Kelly that the GAA managed to distance itself from politics and survived.

The first All-Ireland finals were held in 1887 when Thurles, representing county Tipperary beat Meelick from county Galway in hurling, and Commercials (Limerick) overcame New Irelanders (Louth) in football. Early competitions were awkward affairs, due to a rule where counties could appeal results to the Association's Central Council, which often resulted in lengthy delays.

A new constitution drawn up in 1895 and a gradual healing of political splits meant that by the time Cusack died in 1906, four years after Archbishop Croke, he had left behind a united organisation with a cohesive administrative structure that grew directly into the GAA of today.

chapter three

politics and controversy

Given the nature of its ethos and aims - the promotion of Irish sport and culture - it is perhaps inevitable that politics and the GAA would be frequent bedfellows. Although this was particularly true in the early years, the major contemporary issues centre more and more around the games themselves. However, a continuing ban on members of the Northern Ireland security forces ensures that the vestiges of a politicised sporting body remain, and are likely to do so for some time to come.

the ban

Perhaps the ultimate irony of an issue which was more divisive than any other in the history of the GAA is the manner in which it was laid to rest. After sixty years of contentious, often fractious debate, the ban on members of the Association participating in other sports was deleted from the rule book amidst an utter lack of fuss at the annual Congress of 1971 in Belfast.

The Ban, as it was simply referred to, was introduced into the Official Guide, the GAA's constitution, in 1902. The reason for its initial existence was a fear among the Association's leadership that the creeping Anglicisation of Irish sport, culture and politics would, if left unchecked, become hugely detrimental to the future of Gaelic games. Rather than compete on a level playing field with soccer and rugby, the Association felt it could not rely solely on the patriotic instincts of its members. The

Liam McCarthy Cup • Sam Maguire Cup

motion written into the rulebook at Congress of that year read:

"Any member of the Association who plays or encourages in any way rugby, football, hockey or any imported game which is calculated to injuriously affect our National Pastimes, is suspended from the Association".

The Ban provoked disharmony, and was a permanent figure on the agenda for Congress until a motion was passed allowing it to be discussed once every three years. It survived numerous attempts to remove it over the decades until the first major breakthrough came in 1968. A proposal from the Mayo county board to set up a committee to examine the rule and draw up a report stating reasons for the Ban's continued existence was adopted. Comprised of four pro Ban and two anti Ban members, the committee got to work and the report was duly circulated to all clubs by the end of 1970. By the time Congress came around the following year, twenty eight of the thirty two county conventions had already voted to remove it.

Amid a tense, but quiet gathering in Belfast, President Pat Fanning called on a county which favoured abolition to propose the motion. For a few seconds, there was silence around the hall until Armagh delegate Con Shortt stood up and made the proposal. He was quickly seconded by Tom Woulfe of Dublin, whereupon Fanning declared that Rule 27 ceased to exist. Without even a show of hands or the histrionics which had been expected, the Ban was gone.

RULE 21

When the accusation of being a quasi-political body is levelled at the GAA, it is usually referring to Rule 21 which prohibits members of the Royal Ulster Constabulary and British defence forces from participating in Gaelic games. It also forbids GAA members from attending social functions hosted by the RUC or British forces. For a sporting organisation, it is indeed a bizarre diktat. Yet in common with its predecessor on imported games, it has proved more than adept at surviving attempts to scrap it. This is because the rule attracts significant levels of support among delegates from Ulster, whose eloquence in debate on the subject has often swung the minds of the undecided.

The irony of Rule 21 is that, in practical terms, it is almost irrelevant. Were it removed, it is unlikely that either RUC or British army members would have any interest in joining, while

by nature of geography, it only applies to six of the thirty two counties in any case. But a number of factors, including the security forces' often over-zealous approach to keeping tabs on GAA members and the continuing presence of the British army on the property of Crossmaglen Rangers in south Armagh, have hindered greatly any chance of its removal. In Crossmaglen, a considerable proportion of the Association's ground has been requisitioned by the army and a helicopter base stands directly behind the goals. Members of the club complain frequently about games being disrupted by low-flying craft, or balls which stray over the wire not being returned.

During the IRA's ceasefire in 1994, a breakthrough looked

likely when Down became the first Northern county to propose abolition at Congress. It was decided that the matter would be deferred to a special Congress, which, at time of writing, has yet to be set up.

Critics said that the GAA bottled out, missing their best ever opportunity to ditch Rule 21. The subsequent breakdown of the ceasefire in 1996 may have proved them right.

ROUGh STUFF

A strong seam of physicality has always run through Gaelic games. While many individuals have prospered despite lack of stature, compensating with speed and skill, no team has ever been consistently successful without a fair quota of burly engine-room types unafraid to 'mix-it' when the occasion demands.

In football particularly, frequent physical contact is a major element. Inevitably, as with rugby, Australian rules and, to a lesser degree, soccer, on-field violence is the result. Considering both the rules of the game and disciplinary procedures, it can be said that the Association has been somewhat lax in coming to terms with this. Incidents of fisticuffs have been common throughout the GAA's history, but in recent times particularly, the sport's image has paid the price through serious incidents in high-profile, televised games. Of these, the two that stand out most were the All-Ireland football finals of 1983 and 1996.

In 1983, Dublin and Galway met in a decider that remains in the memory for reasons far less attractive than the quality of the

football. In all, four players were sent off in a vicious encounter which led to public outrage unprecedented in the GAA's history.

A swirling wind on the day had put paid to hopes of good football. Dublin, playing with the gale, had the early advantage but the niggly, sour opening exchanges between the sides did not promise a good game. Referee John Gough of Antrim opted for the decisive approach, sensing the mood, and sent off Dublin's Brian Mullins midway through the first half. Ten minutes later, his team mate Ray Hazeley and Galway's Tomas Tierney followed after a spot of off-the-ball wrestling. In an atmosphere of ugly tension the game continued. During half-time, Galway midfielder Brian Talty was attacked in the dressing room tunnel and could not continue.

After the re-start, Dublin's Ciaran Duff became the fourth player for an early bath when a wild swing narrowly missed Pat O'Neill's head, and Dublin were down to twelve men against Galway's fourteen. Amazingly, Galway lost the game, their strategy disintegrating as Dublin dug in, holding on by 1-10 to 1-8.

Media reaction was negative, and the GAA contributed to dragging the whole thing out by insisting on the usual laborious disciplinary proceedings. In the event, a total of two years in suspensions were handed out, Dublin bearing the brunt, but the true price was paid in the tarnished image of the game which was slow to leave the minds of the public.

In 1996, the replay between Meath and Mayo looked like a recipe for trouble. The drawn game had been a scrappy affair, Mayo feeling cheated after Meath equalised late, and there was general ill feeling between the two camps. Early into the replay, the tension erupted as a brawl involving sixteen players broke out near the Hill 16 goal. The madness continued for about two minutes, after which referee Pat McEneaney, at a loss what to do, sent off Colm Coyle of Meath and Mayo's Liam McHale. As with 1983, the aftermath was long and bitter, ending with the suspension of 15 players, and bans totalling 38 months.

Chapter Four

The Greats

Few terms are more roundly abused in sporting contexts than that of *legend*. In Gaelic games, a fresh crop comes every summer. For many their period in bloom is brief, forgotten outside of their own counties with the passing of time and their names added to the lengthy list of those who stood up for their fifteen minutes of fame.

A fair ground rule for assessing the degree to which tags such as hero or legend are deserved is the longevity of their fame. Few indeed are those players whose names remain on the lips of the people long after their heyday has passed.

Any list of the greats of Gaelic games will, almost by definition, be as notable for absentees as for those included. Arguments over the best ever players have whiled away barstool hours for generations and will continue to do so for as long as there is football and hurling to be talked about. Due to the nature of personal selectivity, the following sections make little or no mention of such names as the Rackard brothers of Wexford, the Doyles of Tipperary, Iggy Jones of Tyrone, or Cork's Jimmy Barry Murphy - all greats in their own rights.

But of those who have been included, no one could argue their right to be called the greatest players ever.

FOOTBALL – MICK O'CONNELL, KERRY.

It is more than fitting that Kerry, the cradle of footballing civilisation, should have produced perhaps the game's finest ever exponent. Mick O'Connell came from Valentia, an island tucked into the Kerry coast, battered by the Atlantic and connected to the mainland by bridge.

Tall and possessed of wiry strength, O'Connell was to many who saw him in his heyday in the 1960's the complete footballer. Equally proficient on either right or left foot, his control of the ball was astounding, as were his skills of anticipation. Though not particularly slight of stature, the physical aspect of his game was rarely evident, and thorough sportsmanship and fair play were his hallmarks throughout his career. Contemporary observers noted that unlike most good players who experience the occasional off-day, O'Connell almost never had a bad game. Playing from centre-half-forward, he was the lynchpin for Kerry's three All-Ireland successes of the 1960s, in a team which included Mick O'Dwyer, who would go on to become the most successful manager in the history of the sport.

His intercounty career began in the late 1950s, an explosive display in the All-Ireland final of 1959 against Dublin marking him out for greatness. In all he collected four winners medals in 1959, 1962, 1969 and 1970.

KEVIN HEFFERNAN, DUBLIN, & MICK O DWYER, KERRY.

In the early 1970s, the concept of teams moulded by the strong will and tactical nous of a manager was alien to Gaelic games. Most counties laboured under the constraints of a laboriously overstaffed selection committee, comprising anything up to eight or nine individuals all throwing in their tuppenny opinions when they sat down to pick the teams. Naturally, club and regional biases, to say nothing of petty individual prejudices, came into play with some bizarre team sheets resulting.

Two men and two counties changed all this. Although great players in their own right, the duo whose influence shaped the modern game of Gaelic football did so as managers.

In the late 1970s, Mick O'Dwyer's Kerry and Kevin Heffernan's Dublin changed the face of football irrevocably with what were probably the two greatest teams ever to grace Croke Park. The duels between the pair remain as vivid today as they did twenty years ago and football since has rarely reached such peaks.

The common factor in the approach of both managers was their attitude to fitness. Previously, training methods had changed little for decades and a near uniform level of fitness for most of the top teams was accepted. O'Dwyer and Heffernan upped the ante considerably and produced sides fitter and more mobile than ever seen before. They also both took advantage of a lax hand-passing rule to develop a lightning-fast running game which, though it displeased the purists, made for exhilarating viewing.

Between 1974 and 1979, Dublin and Kerry met five times in successive championship seasons, producing some of the most memorable moments in football history. The record shows that O'Dwyer came out on top, with three victories to two, and

Mick Mackey

subsequent triumphs in the mid 1980s sealed his position as the greatest coach of all time. He was also a revolutionary in terms of waking the GAA up to the possibilities of commercialism, though he received scant praise for it at the time.

Heffernan quit the Dublin job in 1986, O'Dwyer leaving Kerry three years later to take the helm at Kildare. Between them, they left a legacy of greatness which successive managers have never emulated.

HURLING – MICK MACKEY, LIMERICK.

As befits the fastest field game on earth, hurling has always attracted its fair share of flamboyant characters. Perhaps the original and best of these was Mick Mackey. Mackey was probably the first superstar in Gaelic games. Tall, dark, dashing and charismatic, he captured the attention of an adoring public from the moment he first played in the colours of Limerick in 1934. Mackey was born in Castleconnell and spent all his playing days at centre-forward for the Ahane club. Though always utilised in a scoring role, he was renowned for tremendous versatility and a bewildering variety of strokes.

Blessed with balance and the grace of a gazelle, his tendency towards hurtling for goal with the ball on his stick made him a natural crowd pleaser. Aside from his outstanding individual talents, Mackey also had the good fortune to be around for a golden age of Limerick hurling. Between 1934 and 1940 Limerick won three All-Irelands and lost another narrowly, a level of success which has yet to be repeated in Limerick's history.

In his first year as an inter-county player, Mackey was thrown in at the deep end. Limerick reached the All-Ireland final against a battling Dublin side in the GAA's Jubilee year of 1934. At the age of twenty two he lined out with his brother John, also a player of some distinction, in the half-forward line but Limerick could only manage to draw the first encounter before winning out 5-2 to 2-6 in a replay.

Mackey was outstanding in the following year, cutting a swathe through opposing defences as Limerick beat the best in Munster to qualify for another final, this time against Kilkenny.

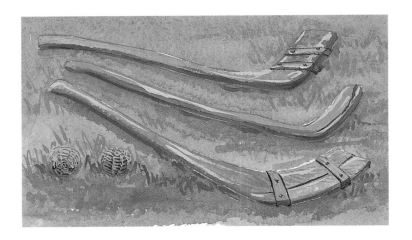

Trailing by a point in the final moments, Mackey won a free at close range and instead of putting it over the bar to tie the match, threw caution to the wind and went for goal. The shot was saved and Limerick lost.

From that day in 1935 to the Munster final of 1937, the county were unbeaten. At the height of his powers in 1936, Mackey scored an amazing five goals and three points as Tipperary were overcome in the Munster decider. Limerick went on to revenge the defeat against Kilkenny of a year earlier by handing out a 13-point drubbing in the All-Ireland final. It took three years to reach Croke Park again, where Kilkenny once more provided the opposition in the final. Limerick won by 3-2 to 1-7 in what was to be Mackey's last All-Ireland title. Added to these, he won seven Railway Cup titles in the colours of Munster at a time when the competition enjoyed far greater distinction than it does today.

Christy Ring

In September 1982 at the age of seventy, Mick Mackey died. In the churchyard of Castleconnell, a crowd of thousands assembled to mourn the last of the true cavaliers from the golden age of hurling in the Thirties, Forties and Fifties. With Cork legend Christy Ring having died prematurely in 1979, Mackey's death sounded the final whistle for what most devotees of the game consider its heyday.

—CHRISTY RING, CORK

Christy Ring is to hurling what Ali is to boxing, Jessie Owens is to athletics, or Pele is to soccer. As close to a definition of perfection as his sport has ever come. The records he set during an amazing intercounty career which spanned over two decades still stand to this day - eight All-Ireland winners' medals (equalled only by Tipperary's John Doyle) and eighteen Railway Cup winners' medals with a scoring record of 42 goals and 105 points from his forty four appearances in the interprovincial competition.

Yet statistics go nowhere near to providing an explanation of the phenomenon that was 'Ringey'. His appeal to crowds was magnetic, in Cork he was the figurehead of a worshipful cult. His name on a teamsheet was enough to guarantee a full house and the battles for supremacy between Cork and Tipperary of the 1950s in which he played so prominent a role have long passed into legend.

Unlike the tall and swarthy Mackey, Ring was shorter and more squatly built. But he had tremendous power in his wrists and arms and could send a ball flying with the merest flick. His opponents spoke of him as being completely unpredictable, with no set pattern to his game and no way of anticipating what he would do next. Allied to this was a hunger to win and a lifelong obsession with hurling. When asked what stood him apart from other hurlers, Ring once reflected, with massive understatement, that he "had a great determination when going for the ball". More accurately, brick walls would have been but a trifling obstacle between Ring and the goalmouth.

His first All-Ireland success was in 1941, the first of Cork's four-in-a-row. He captained the county on three successful campaigns in 1946, 1953 and 1954. Much of Cork's success in that era is directly credited to Ring and the inspirational effects he had on his team mates. The battles for supremacy in Munster against Tipperary generally brought out the best in his combative nature; during the 1950s, Cork and Tipperary shared six All-Irelands between them and their near-annual meetings in Limerick for the Munster final are regarded as among the greatest games ever played.

Ring played on for Cork until 1962. A year later, the Cork selectors voted 3-2 not to select him, but amazingly, at the age of 46, he was called back onto the panel and selected as a sub, 33-year-old John Bennett being preferred.

"The people of Cork will never see the day when Christy Ring is a sub on a Cork team to John Bennett," he declared haughtily when withdrawing his services, as ever, second-best to nobody.

After retiring from his playing career, Ring was a selector on the Cork side which won three successive All-Irelands from 1976-78. He died prematurely at the age of 58 in March 1979.

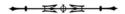

ChAPTER FIVE

GREAT GAMES AND RIVALRIES

DUBLIN V KERRY, 1975-86

When Kevin Heffernan was appointed manager in 1973, Dublin, a county with the proudest of traditions, were at an all-time low. They hadn't reached a Leinster final since 1965. After a mere four months in charge, the Heffernan reformation was well in place and Dublin won the All-Ireland in 1974 against Galway.

In Kerry, Mick O'Dwyer took the helm in 1975 with a glittering eighteen year career in the county colours behind him. Despite the fact that only five years had passed since Kerry had won two-in-a-row, an air of gloom pervaded in a county where success is regarded as a birthright.

Both managers took over teams at a low ebb; no-one could have predicted the extent to which they would build teams whose legacy of rivalry will live forever in the folklore of the Gaelic games.

The first in a series of annual clashes which would last until the end of the decade, came in 1975. It also marked the beginning of a fascinating psychological duel between the two managers, who went to great lengths in their efforts to outwit one another tactically.

Kerry lost captain Mickey O'Sullivan early in the game, but instead of throwing their rhythm, it seemed to spur them to greater heights. They ran out winners on a scoreline of 2-12 to 0-11 amidst much hyperbole about the 'greatest Kerry team ever" and such like. But Heffernan learned the lesson well. With a brand new half-back line of Pat O'Neill, Tommy Drumm and Kevin Moran, later to go on to international stardom in soccer with Manchester United and the Republic of Ireland, the Dubs turned Kerry over a year later.

The new additions succeeded in choking the quick-passing game on which Kerry depended, while at the other end, the Dublin forwards mesmerised their opponents with innovative angles of attack. They ran out comfortable winners on a scoreline of 3-8 to 0-10.

In 1977 the pair were drawn to meet in the All-Ireland semi-final and produced one of the greatest games of all time. Played at electrifying pace with flowing passing movements executed to perfection, Kerry stayed in the lead until the final six minutes. But Dublin saved the killer blow until late when two goals from David Hickey and Bernard Brogan gave them a five-point victory amidst euphoric scenes. They went on to comfortably dispose of Armagh in the final.

For Dublin, it represented the pinnacle of their powers. A year later Mick O'Dwyer, having survived immense dissatisfaction at successive years of failure at home, brought his team back to Croke Park with an intense determination to settle the score. Both Kerry and Dublin had destroyed all opposition en route to the final.

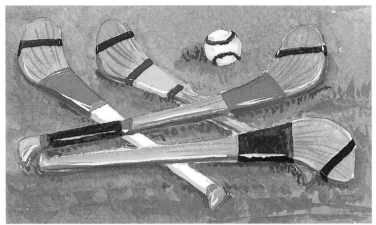

Despite Dublin's two-in-a-row in 1976-77, it is the final of 1978 which is considered the defining moment in the rivalry. With their customary bravado, the Dubs built up an early lead but a John Egan goal restored Kerry's chances in the match. There then followed perhaps the most infamous goal in All-Ireland history. Kerry were awarded a free on the 21 yard line, and Dublin keeper Paddy Cullen ran out of his goal to remonstrate with the referee. Sensing the opportunity, Mikey Sheehy took a quick, deft chip to the net as Cullen, his face a mask of horror, backpedalled furiously to no avail. There followed an inexplicable Dublin collapse. Spurred on by their new full-forward, Eoin 'Bomber' Liston who plundered three second-half goals, Kerry won by the huge margin of 5-11 to 0-9, the biggest since 1946. For the Dublin team which had triumphed gladitorially in the two previous years, it was nothing short of ignominious.

Although they returned the following year after bruising wins over Offaly in Leinster and Roscommon in the semi-final, Dublin were miles away from their former selves and again succumbed crushingly in the final: 3-13 to 1-8.

For Kerry, there were no more heights to be reached. Their reign extended until 1982, when they attempted an unprecedented five titles in a row. Although beaten in successive years, by Offaly in 1982 and by Cork in the Munster championship of 1983, they came back to win another three-in-a-row from 1984-86, vanquishing Dublin under Heffernan twice more before their era of glory came to a close.

OFFALY V KERRY, 1982
1-15   0-17

A quick glance in the bookmakers' windows the week before the All-Ireland final of 1982 served well to illustrate the enormity of Offaly's achievement. Kerry, undisputed champions and seeming unbeatable in the Championship competition were 1-4/ to become the first team in history to win five consecutive All-Ireland titles. Offaly, by contrast, had been beaten by Kerry in the previous two finals and were generally considered to lack the strength in depth to cope with a sustained Kerry onslaught.

The Offaly manager that year was Eugene McGee. Although he lacked the background of a distinguished playing career, he was a master strategist with an intimate knowledge of the game's more subtle nuances.

The All Ireland of 1982 was regarded as Offaly's last chance at winning the Championship. The team had reached its peak and probably would have cracked up under the strain of a third successive All-Ireland defeat. In the final, McGee resisted the urge to play defensively, having noted that Kerry liked nothing better than taking apart teams who attempted to stifle them. He built his team around a solid spine of Sean Lowry at centre-back, Ritchie Connor at centre-forward and the prolific Matt Connor at number 14.

The game was tight throughout, but when the post-mortems were carried out later, many in Kerry blamed Mikey Sheehy for a first-half penalty miss. At the time it looked irrelevant as Kerry went on to build up a four-point lead. Two points from Matt Connor had halved that, but with only ninety seconds remaining, Kerry's victory looked inevitable.

Offaly had introduced substitute Seamus Darby earlier on with general instructions to hang around the goal area - a command which proved extremely fortuitous. His winning goal provoked a storm of controversy as to whether or not he had pushed Tommy Doyle before gaining possession. But in any event, he tucked it away to put Offaly into a one-point lead to which they clung until the final whistle. For Kerry, it was the most painful defeat in their history, exaggerated by the fact that no one had even contemplated anything less than the five-in-a-row. For McGee and Offaly, it was a vindication for a team which had refused to lie down in the face of staggering odds.

2-11   2-7

The final of 1947 remains significant as the only decider ever to be played outside of Ireland. With World War II and the lean years which accompanied it at an end, there was a pervasive feeling of optimism and adventure within the Association. A year earlier, a request from the New York board to host the football final replay between Kerry and Roscommon had been rejected out of hand, but by the time Congress met in early 1947, the idea was gaining momentum. Also, it was the centenary of *Black '47*, the worst year in the Irish potato famine, and it was thought fitting that the emigrants who left Ireland in their droves at that time should be commemorated.

Two delegates were sent to New York to report on the feasibility of staging the final there and on their return, Congress voted 20-17 in favour of the project, with the proviso that Central Council were to retain full control of the organisation. Cavan and Kerry qualified for the decider, and the whole of Ireland tuned in to hear Michael O'Hehir's radio broadcast from the Polo Grounds.

After fifteen minutes Kerry had scored 2-2 to no score from their opponents. But Cavan made some positional tinkering to great effect and came storming back, using the platform of a half-back line of Duke, Deignan and John Joe Reilly to mount attack after attack. They went on to win by 2-11 to 2-7, with an outstanding forward display by Peter Donohoe, christened in the New York press as 'the Babe Ruth of Gaelic football'. The teams returned to a rapturous reception in October, but the success of the venture was not fully appreciated until that December when the accounts showed a profit of £10,000 from the game.

The greatest significance of the New York All-Ireland was the renewal of the bond with the ex-pat community in America, a link which remains strong to this day despite occasional friction over top players 'weekending' in America without proper clearance from the authorities at home.

CORK V WEXFORD, 1954

1-9   1-6

If the 1970s was the golden age for football, then hurling had its equivalent twenty years earlier. Titanic battles in Munster between Cork and Tipperary drew massive crowds annually to see the exploits of Christy Ring and the Doyles of Tipperary, while in Leinster, the Wexford side containing the precociously talented Rackard brothers, Willie, Nicky and Bobby, reigned supreme.

When the sides met in 1954, it was billed as a direct clash between Ring and the Wexford trio. In the event, it was not one of Ring's better games in a Cork jersey but rather, as the Irish Independent put it the next day, a match in which "every man was utterly unmindful of his personal safety".

Bobby Rackard shone at the heart of the Wexford defence, and Ring, despite being restricted to occasional flashes of his brilliance, still managed five points in a low-scoring encounter.

After twenty five minutes, Tom Ryan scored a goal for Wexford to put them two points ahead. Taking the ball from a sideline cut, he gathered in the square and with space restricting his ability to strike, hand-passed to the net. Wexford opened the brighter in the second half, but Cork were resurrected by a Johnny Clifford goal in the twenty sixth minute to go a point ahead. Further points from Ring and Josie Hartnett put the lid on it for Cork, to the delight of their following in a crowd of 84,856.

chapter six

OVERSEAS

Ireland was never a colonial nation and Gaelic games were never likely to explode on the international scene in the same way that soccer, cricket and rugby did.

Emigration from Ireland was common as thousands of men, women and children went into exile to escape social and economic hardship. From the time of the Famine when over a million people left the country to subsequent waves of exiles throughout the twentieth century, thriving Irish communities have sprung up worldwide, and it is these which have given Gaelic games whatever international credentials they possess. However, exile teams have rarely risen to the standard set by home players and remain very much on the periphery of mainstream Gaelic games. Abroad, it is not surprising that Gaelic games are strongest in London and New York, the two biggest centres of Irish diaspora.

London has its own club structure and county sides compete within the main intercounty leagues and championships run from Ruislip. The transient nature of much of the Irish community in England has meant problems in terms of developing consistent teams, but recent successes have included promotion for their hurlers to Division Two of the National League. In general, the majority of the players are Irish born, and the GAA has found it difficult to attract support from first and second-generation immigrants in the face of the thriving English soccer scene.

Other centres in England include Warwickshire and Lancashire. Teams in these counties do not compete at senior level in the Championship, but take part in various junior and intermediate competitions.

Teams in New York operate with a considerable degree of autonomy from headquarters in Dublin - a situation which has often led to tension and conflict between the two sides of the Atlantic.

The New York Board runs a domestic championship based on county representative sides and during the latter stages of the competition, the New York teams tend to recruit heavily from the ranks of Irish based players to bolster their chances. This is deemed illegal under the Association's rules without the proper clearance from relevant county boards, and it can safely be said that there are certain high profile players who have had more pseudonyms than Carlos the Jackal in this regard. Irish players are routinely set up in jobs and accommodation for the summer in return for their services in New York.

On a couple of occasions, famous names caught out playing illegally in New York have caused major embarrassment to the GAA. The most famous of these was Galway's star hurler Tony Keady, who missed the All-Ireland final of 1988 having played a New York championship game without proper clearance. Keady had gone to New York with Galway on a tour and stayed on to play a couple of games with Laois (county allegiances are irrelevant in the context of the New York competition).

Although Keady claimed he was under the impression that all relevant paperwork had been processed by Laois officials, this was not the case. An objection was launched in New York and the board there banned Keady for two games which mattered little as by this time he was back home where the suspension did not apply. However Croke Park's Games Administration Committee launched its own investigation, after which Keady and two other Galway players - Aidan Staunton and Michael Helebert - were banned for a year.

Galway at that time were due to play Tipperary in the All-Ireland hurling semi-final and were incensed that one of their star players, the other two being relatively minor figures, would miss the game in such a manner. In fact, they seriously considered withdrawing from the fixture, prompting the GAA to call a special meeting of Central Council on the Tuesday before the semi-final to discuss an appeal. But Council turned down Keady's plea on a vote of 20-18. Without him, Galway managed

to have another two players sent off in the semi-final and lost by three points. To add insult to injury, the GAA declared an amnesty for New York 'illegals' who came forward and confessed later that year, naturally leaving Galway and Keady somewhat miffed.

Eight years later the scandal was repeated on a massive scale when up to 20 intercounty players were caught playing illegally. Reacting to an Irish problem with an Irish solution, the GAA first dished out heavy suspensions with much solemn talk, before commuting them all on appeal.

The other principal centres of Gaelic games in America are Philadelphia, Chicago and San Francisco, which are separate from the New York Board and operate under the auspices of the North American Board, which has close ties to the GAA's administration in Ireland.

Away from America, the most high profile international venture the GAA indulged in recently was the Compromise Rules Series with the Australian Football League. Although Australian Rules Football was originally formulated as a pastime to keep cricketers fit during the winter months, it owes much to Gaelic football. Both games are fifteen a side with goals as well as points, both employ the hand-pass and much of the fielding and general play are broadly similar. Therefore coming up with an agreed set of rules proved easy enough and the first series took place in Ireland in the GAA's centenary year of 1984. The Irish had won a major concession when it was decided to use a round ball instead of the oval Australian version and despite being pitted against full-time professionals, the home side won the Test series 2-1.

The games were also noted for a number of memorable brawls, sparked by the Australian's habitually more physical game and Irish misinterpretations of a rather robust tackling technique. Despite this, three subsequent series followed both in Ireland and Australia, the last of these being in 1990 when Ireland won convincingly away from home and the Aussies decided that round footballs were definitely not for them. Since then there has been occasional talk of a revival, but interest at top level has never amounted to much.

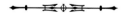

chapter seven

The Future

Croke Park's New Stand rises in a shimmer of concrete and steel on the north Dublin skyline, a testament to the spirit of change in the GAA as the end of the millennium approaches. By the year 2010, the gradual re-development of Headquarters will be complete; an all-seater stadium housing 80,000 with extensive corporate hospitality facilities. Amazingly, for an amateur body, the Association hopes to complete the project without incurring debt.

Well over a century after its foundation, the Association is only now beginning to discover the true financial potential of Gaelic games. While solvency has rarely been a problem, the iron-clad ethos of amateurism often led to issues such as sponsorship, corporatism and even marketing being viewed with a considerable degree of suspicion.

Nowadays, both the football and hurling championships attract massive sponsorship deals, as well as television rights being sold around the globe to the multitudes of Irish ex-patriate communities. Though determined to safeguard the universal availability of terrestrial television, the Association has initiated deals with satellite and cable channels for highlight programmes: an aspect certain to develop further in the coming years.

The corporate facilities in the new Croke Park have proved successful, providing the Association with a principal source of

finance for the reconstruction work, while vast improvements on spectator facilities are used to justify considerable price-hikes in entry fees for big games. In financial terms, the future looks as bright as can be imagined. The remarkable aspect is the short period of time in which such a change in the culture of the GAA has been implemented.

Until the 1990s, teams were forbidden to wear a sponsor's logo on jerseys, and only in 1997 were the strict rules on individual players earning money through endorsements and appearances relaxed. They are still forbidden to employ their own agents to such ends. Even twenty years ago, such innovations would have been looked upon with horror, but it is a measure of the more tolerant climate towards moneymaking activities that full professionalism is now openly discussed, even though it looks unlikely in the near future.

Pay-for-play is a concept abhorrent to traditionalists. However, the increasing demands on the time of top-level footballers and hurlers make it inevitable. At peak season, top teams would not consider training less than five nights a week. For some, additional sessions in the early morning before the working day begins are also the norm. The GAA has always depended on employers' generosity with their staff's time, but as average fitness levels spiral ever-upwards, being an inter-county footballer or hurler is little short of a full-time occupation.

With many, the strain is starting to show and demands for increased expense allowances and more freedom to cash in on fame via promotional work have grown to a cacophony. Changes to regulations regarding this have been slow in coming, but there has been a relaxation on the rules regarding a player's freedom to profit from a high public profile.

As regards activities on the playing fields, a stark contrast has emerged between football and hurling in the 1990s. Although the hallmark of the decade in both sports has been the emergence of champions away from the traditional power bases, the development of the games has been vastly different. Although purists will argue that skill levels are nowhere near what they once were, top-level hurling in general has become faster and perhaps more exciting than ever before. The public has responded accordingly, and gate receipts for championship and league games have rocketed. Reforms introduced in 1996 have meant the season is now run off between March and October, scrapping competitive hurling during the winter months when bad weather and soggy ground often led to a less than exhilarating spectacle for players and supporters alike. The setting up of a Hurling Development Committee has been a huge success, combating effectively what was a trend towards decline outside the sport's traditional heartlands. Whereas only a few years ago the prophets of doom were forecasting the marginalisation of hurling into a minority sport, confined to rural pockets, the prognosis now is more akin to a dawning of a golden age of popularity for this oldest of games.

Where football is concerned, the heydays of the late 1970s seem but a distant memory. Unlike hurling, which has incorporated new levels of fitness into its traditionally more skill-based ethos, the more subtle aspects of football have suffered immensely. A growing trend towards physicality threatens to wipe out the kind of running, flowing game perfected by the great Dublin and Kerry teams in favour of a more hit-and-run affair, with most games being decided on scores from free-kicks. In the 1990s, a string of pretty poor All-Ireland finals from 1994 onwards have highlighted this starkly, culminating in the replay between Meath and Mayo in 1996 which degenerated into a mass brawl early in the first half. Such scenes, broadcast around the world, have been detrimental to say the least in persuading parents to encourage children to take up Gaelic games.

But there are signs that the GAA is taking steps to restore the game to its former glories. Congress of 1997 set up a Football Development Committee with a sweeping mandate to

recommend changes in the entire structure of the game, and initial indications are that this is exactly what it will do. Whereas the hurling equivalent set out to strengthen and develop the game at its grass roots, it seems likely that the football committee will attempt to alter radically, through rule changes and strict disciplinary procedures, the entire culture of a game fast becoming dragged down in a mire of physicality. The committee's report is due in the autumn of 1997.

As an organisation, the GAA has always been slow in changing its ways - a natural byproduct of the innate rural conservatism which make up its grass roots. But while maintaining a distinctly Irish identity, there are palpable signs of an evolution within the Association towards a more open, cosmopolitan outlook. The suspicion with which other sports have always been viewed is diminishing somewhat - it is increasingly common for top players to spend their winters playing soccer and summers playing Gaelic - and even the most hardline diktats such as Rule 21 stand a fair chance of being consigned to the dustbin of history as the new Millennium approaches.

But for all the controversies and occasional posturing, the GAA can look ahead with huge optimism. As long as those for whom the year revolves around the sound of clashing ash and the roar of a summer's crowd, the unique position of the games in the hearts and minds of Irish people can never be removed.